MW00984883

A

BEGINNER'S GUIDE TO PRACTICING

SCRIPTURAL IMAGINATION

———

KENNETH H. CARTER JR.

UPPER ROOM BOOKS®
NASHVILLE

Cover design: Bruce Gore | Gore Studio
Cover imagery: Shutterstock
Typesetting and interior design: PerfecType | Nashville, TN

ISBNs
978-0-8358-1918-3 (print)
978-0-8358-1919-0 (mobi)
978-0-8358-1920-6 (ePub)

Printed in the United States of America

*In memory of my mother, Frieda; and with gratitude
for my granddaughter, Paige; and with
sure trust and confidence that the scriptures will
speak to us, from generation to generation*

Contents

————

Introduction:
A Beginner's Guide to
Practicing Scriptural Imagination

———

My purpose in writing this brief volume is to focus on four passages of scripture that can contribute to our growth as followers of Jesus:

- The Vine and the Branches (John 15:1-17)
- The Sower, the Seed, and the Soils (Mark 4:1-9)
- The Feeding of the Multitudes (Luke 9:10-17)
- The Parable of the Talents (Matthew 25:14-30)

The intention is that these passages and reflections on them will be read in community—in a home or a coffee shop, in a church classroom or a pub. This community might be established, such as the gathering of close friends over a sustained period of time in a small group or Sunday school class. Or its members may be coming to know one another. The church is more than a gathering of persons within the walls of our buildings. There is an increasing need for gatherings of friends and strangers beyond the walls of our churches. And yet, once we are there, how is growth nurtured? How do we become disciples?

I have lived for some time with these four passages of scripture, and each includes lessons about spiritual growth and development, how we are formed to live more graciously, and how we resist the obstacles—the "fightings without, and fears within" (UMH, no. 553; see also 2 Corinthians 7:5)—to this process. And yet, through it all, the God who began a good work in us, the apostle Paul writes, will be faithful to complete it (see Philippians 1:6). The initial gift of grace, present in every person, is honored through attention to the means (channels) of God's presence—the scriptures, prayers, conversation and listening, testimony, mutual encouragement, and accountability. These channels of God's grace, ordinary and extraordinary, contain the current of a powerful and ever-present stream of the divine revelation. At times, if we are attentive, we will sense that something is happening in our midst; Jesus called this the kingdom (or reign) of God (see Mark 1:15).

This book is intended as a basic *catechesis* (a Greek word for instruction or preparation) for participants to explore these biblical texts and as an additional guide for seasoned leaders to think through their callings in a mixed ecology of church. A "mixed ecology of church" refers to the presence of both traditional and new forms of church. The church has become weighed down by industrial, bureaucratic, and institutional structure, which can require much of our time and energy. Some larger congregations are indeed strong and flourishing; Elaine Heath has described these as "anchor" churches, which give life beyond themselves to smaller communities. The necessity of a "both/and" way forward creates contexts for a study group within a larger church—a church within a church (*ecclesiola in ecclesia*) or a new form of church that meets in a setting beyond the walls of our buildings. By definition, a "fresh expression" of church is

> a form of church for our changing culture, established primarily for the benefit of people who are not yet members of any church. . . . It will come into being through principles of listening, service, incarnational [contextual] mission and making disciples. . . . It will have the potential to become a mature expression of church *shaped by the gospel* and the enduring marks of the church and for its cultural context.[1]

These four scripture passages are intended to begin—or continue—the process of *shaping persons by the gospel* for the larger purpose of creating Christian community (the church) and transforming the world. And, of course, the scriptures are intended to be read in community with others. As Ellen F. Davis and Richard B. Hays note, "Faithful interpretation of Scripture invites and presupposes participation in the community brought into being by God's redemptive action. That is the church."[2]

Cultivating a Scriptural Imagination

These four passages from the Gospels can help us to grow spiritually, particularly as we cultivate a scriptural imagination that forms us in knowing more about the text and the world, the neighborhood and the networks that we inhabit. Richard Hays describes a scriptural imagination as

> the capacity to see the world through lenses given to us in Scripture—but when we see the world through such lenses, it doesn't just change the way we see the contemporary world but also changes the way we see Scripture. There's a hermeneutical circle between the reading of the text and the reading of the world in which we find ourselves.[3]

The word *hermeneutic* is a Greek word rooted in the experience of our practice of expressing a divine idea in human language—it is about interpreting something with spiritual meaning into a common understanding.

I want to offer five elements of a scriptural imagination.

1. We cultivate a scriptural imagination in community, among a chorus of complementary voices and a diversity of spiritual gifts.

The scriptures are intended to be read in community, with others. This community includes the women and men with whom we gather, and of course they will bring their life experiences, which will at times call for celebration and at other times concern. But the community is also a communion of saints that reaches back in time, to the apostles, martyrs, saints, mystics, prophets, evangelists, and reformers.

We read scripture in a great tradition. And this tradition includes resonant and diverse voices who have much to teach us. As we remember those who have read and lived the scriptures before us, we are immersed in a deep river of insight, courage, and faith: Dietrich Bonhoeffer and Phoebe Palmer, Howard Thurman and Oscar Romero, Thomas á Kempis and Teresa of Avila, John Wesley and Martin Luther. In addition, the community is blessed by a diversity of gifts, and some of us will hear in the scriptures a call to evangelize, others a need for deeper faith, and yet others a burden for service. The community overcomes the limitations of a singular approach to what the scripture might be saying to us. As C. Kavin Rowe notes, "We read alone when we think that Scripture is a matter of the text and me. Scripture, however, was written both to and for Christian communities, and the theological logic of the texts presupposes a community of readers."[4]

2. A scriptural imagination is shaped by the stories of Israel, Jesus, and the early church.

Over time, we are introduced to the scriptures, perhaps through sermons or phrases that we sing in choruses or hymns.

We next begin to see patterns in how God's grace is present in particular verses or passages of scripture or in how we are being called to love our neighbors or bear their burdens. And then, with a greater depth of sustained reading, we become immersed in the larger stories of the Bible—how God creates and liberates us, how God sends prophets to remind us of covenantal relationships and the dream of a more just world, how God is present in suffering and rejoicing, and indeed how God can at times seem very near and at other times absent.

A scriptural imagination is formed by the wholeness of scripture, and over time we discover that the whole of scripture speaks to the wholeness of our lives—our need for healing, occasions for lament, rituals that mark significant transitions in our lives, the very real presence of fear, and our capacity to make idols (substitutes) for God. God's faithful presence in the history of Israel; in the life, death, and resurrection of Jesus; and in his ongoing presence and reality in the lives of his gathered disciples provides a powerful framework for our lives and our communities. The whole of scripture becomes the lens through which we see ourselves in relation to the world and to God.

3. A scriptural imagination avoids categories and models that flatten our perspectives and rejects identities that we privilege above how we are named in scripture.

A scriptural imagination has the power to ground us in broader communal and cultural conversations. It occurs to me that almost every significant question and problem facing us—from poverty to immigration to human sexuality to climate change to privilege—would benefit from men and women who sit before biblical texts, listening for what God might be saying, and who sit just as attentively before the people they (we/I) are (are/am) so quick to label, judge, dismiss, or stereotype. The beautiful hermeneutical circle of which Richard Hays speaks is the Word becoming flesh (see John 1:14). When judgment is premature, the Word remains a word. There may be some small merit to others or value within us in the self-expression, but there is no change. When our way of reading scripture never changes and when our way of seeing the neighbor or the world never changes, the scriptures are not the dynamic Word of God for us. We are not reading them the way the Holy Spirit intended—to convict, to guide us into all truth—and God is not glorified (see John 16:8, 13). God is glorified when the church cultivates a scriptural imagination. And when disciples cultivate a scriptural imagination, the world is transformed.

4. A scriptural imagination is nourished in silence and meditation.

"Be still," the Lord speaks through the psalmist, "and know that I am God" (Ps. 46:10). To hear the still small voice of God, we will need times and spaces that are set apart from the soundtrack of noise and distraction that is a constant in many of our lives. For some, this will be a pattern of reading scripture early in the morning; for others, late at night. We may search intentionally for a space that is quiet—a park, restaurant, coffee shop, or the exercise of walking or running.

When we begin to develop a habit of silence before the scriptures and meditation on them, we discover an abundance of resources in the Christian tradition for nourishing a scriptural imagination—Centering Prayer, *lectio divina* ("divine reading"), Quaker silence, the Jesuit *Examen*. Each of these practices can serve as a model for a deeper, slower, and more focused attentiveness to scripture. The discipline is an unhurried listening to what God is saying to us through a passage of scripture, through a verse, or even through a word. The aim is less rather than more, quality rather than quantity, humility rather than mastery. And over time, the result is a more intimate relationship with God.

5. A scriptural imagination moves beyond information to formation, beyond exposure to immersion.

Spiritual formation is not a goal that we achieve, a body of knowledge that we master, such as a certificate or an academic degree. Instead, as Kavin Rowe suggests, it is

> a way of being in the world that evidences a life-long process of transformation by the power of holy Scripture. [This way of being] is not simply a matter of "thinking"; nor is it only a "doing." Such dichotomies between thought and practice, in fact,

hinder our ability to be scripturally shaped precisely because they teach us to conceive of our lives as divisible things. But human lives are not divisible; insofar as they are human lives, they are unified by the thing that is the human being through time. All of our thought takes place within the lives that we live, and our practices are inseparably intertwined with the thinking that makes the practices intelligible. Scripture aims at the formation of the total pattern that is the way we are in the world—thought and practice together in one life.[5]

Both Hays and Rowe point to a way of reading and living scripture, how we see the world and how we inhabit that world, and how our spiritual practice (such as reading scripture) shapes and is shaped by our actions. The process of forming a scriptural imagination leads to a more integrated life—our thinking influencing our daily habits and practices, and our daily habits and practices influencing our thinking. This is the process of becoming a mature disciple of Jesus Christ, as we take on the mind of Christ (see Philippians 2:5-8) and as we become imitators of him (see 1 Corinthians 11:1). And the fruit of this practice is a greater love for God and our neighbor (see Matthew 22). By this, Jesus taught us, others will know that we are his disciples (see John 13).

This resource contains four basic texts, one from each of the four Gospels. Each is rooted in an organic context; each has the capacity to help us live in a more grounded way before our Creator and one another. Jesus often used the material substances that form the imagery of these scripture passages—soil, vines, branches, bread, the earth, seeds—to guide us in the spiritual life. And, of course, the spiritual life is deeply material, earthy, incarnational. These four texts can help us to grow spiritually, particularly as we cultivate a scriptural imagination that forms us in knowing more about the text and the world, the neighborhood, and the social networks that we inhabit.

So, we will engage with four teachings of Jesus, and in the process, we will develop a scriptural imagination as we *read, reflect, respond,* and then *rest* in the wisdom of the spiritual exercise.

How to Use This Book

———

You are following through on an intention to turn (or return) to the scriptures and to see them as a resource for your own growth as a disciple of Jesus Christ. This is the process of cultivating a scriptural imagination, which is the integration of your thinking, praying, and living, all grounded in the invitation to love God with your heart, soul, and mind, and to love your neighbor as you love yourself (see Matthew 22:37-39).

The heart of this beginner's guide is four chapters, each corresponding to a passage in one of the four Gospels (Matthew, Mark, Luke, John). The following is a simple agenda for reading the Gospels in community, which was how they were originally shared. This plan can be adapted, but it does serve to care for many of the habits that cultivate a scriptural imagination.

Gathering (5 minutes)

Check in with one another and offer a warm welcome. It is important that each person has the opportunity to speak or share in some way that is comfortable and natural to them, and of course this can be a very simple acknowledgment. What is most important is that the members of the community use this time to transition from their everyday lives into a space that is shared and holy.

Prayer for Illumination (3–5 minutes)

The Word is a lamp to our feet and a light to our path (see Psalm 119:105). As you enter into the silence of prayer, ask for the indwelling presence of Jesus Christ, who is the Light of the world, to increase your understanding of the scriptures and to deepen your love for one another.

Scripture Reading (10 minutes)

Let your gathered community know that the Gospel passage will be read twice. Ask one of the participants to slowly read the passage from the Gospel, and ask all present to listen for a word or phrase that resonates with them. Allow a minute for silence. Then ask a different participant to slowly read the passage again, and ask all present to name an idea or concern that they hope will become part of the agenda for conversation. Ask one group member to record these responses.

Conversation and Listening (20 minutes)

Once these ideas and concerns are listed, begin to explore what the Gospel is saying in the group. How are you being called to grow spiritually? How are you being called to live in relation to one another? How are you being called to engage your community? How is God seeking to change or transform your mind? How is God seeking to change or transform your behaviors?

Calling and Sending Forth (10 minutes)

What is an image from the Gospel that has the potential to shape your thinking and living? Where are you in the Gospel? Where is your community in the Gospel? Is the Lord calling you to respond with a specific gift, or is the Lord confronting you with a matter you have been seeking to avoid? Naming the ways in which you are being called and sent is an act of courage and vulnerability.

Prayers of Intercession and Gratitude (10 minutes)

In a circle, share any needs that are present in the community. If possible, express these needs in the language of the Gospel that has been at the center of the group's reflection. Ask a participant to gather these requests in a few sentences, and offer them to God as an act of dependence and trust.

As a concluding act, give thanks for the triune God, who is the source of our lives, and for the gift of Christian community.

1

The Vine and the Branches

John 15:1-17

Connection

Jesus says, "I am the vine, and you are the branches . . . and apart from me you can do nothing" (John 15:5, adapted). He is talking about growth, life, connection. The visible strength of the branches comes from a source, the vine. "Apart from me," Jesus says, "you can do nothing." At the core of Christianity is the assumption that we have a spiritual need. To be a Christian is to trust that God overcomes our weaknesses, forgives our failures, heals our brokenness.

We can live in connection with the God who wants to give us grace, help, forgiveness, salvation. There *is* a human temptation to keep God at a distance. And yet, to be a Christian is to admit that we need a Savior; it is to say, "I cannot do this on my own." Here is the good news: When we ask for help, we discover that God's grace is present in our weakness and that this grace is sufficient. The 12-step approach would say it this way: *When we confess that we are powerless, we are connected with an incredible power.* "Apart from me, you can do nothing," Jesus says. "Live in me," he says; "abide with me."

If we read ahead in the story, we are given a further explanation. Jesus says, "I no longer call you servants, but I have called you friends" (John 15:5). To be a Christian is to be a friend of Jesus, to be at home in his presence, to live in him, and to know that he is alive. I'll say this as simply as I know how: We are invited into a friendship with Jesus Christ, to experience this connection.

If we live long enough, we discover the importance of friendships, because in friendships we become aware that we matter to some other person, and so we try to stay connected. How do friends stay connected? Again, simply, we stay in touch. Friends talk, listen, ask questions, come alongside. Friends are genuinely interested; they want to learn about what is going on in each other's lives.

What does a friendship with Jesus look like? There is time to talk and listen. This is *prayer*. A friendship with Jesus is all about prayer. The late Henri Nouwen is said to have met a seeker who seemed to be uncomfortable. He and the woman happened to be seated next to each other at a charity function. Finally, their conversation turned toward the real issue: "I'm having trouble believing in God, in all of this," she said. Nouwen looked into the eyes of the woman, and with intensity he said to her, "Give me five minutes a day, five minutes a day to be silent and in the presence of Jesus . . . five minutes."

We pay attention to our friends. We talk and listen. Could we give five minutes a day to spend in the presence of Jesus? Beyond talking and listening, we ask questions and learn about the lives of our friends. One evening recently, I traveled with a couple of friends to an event that was out of town. Since we had time in the car together, we were able to learn about one another, our hobbies, our children, our work. We laughed. We talked about serious issues, even our political differences! There were silences in the midst of the conversation. A friendship takes that kind of time.

>> **Reflection:** *What qualities, activities and habits do you associate with friendship? How do these carry over into your spiritual life?*

How do we ask questions, how do we learn, in the spiritual life? We turn to the *scriptures*. We open the Bible and take a deep dive into it with our questions, and we begin to learn about this Jesus, who is simple and yet also so mysterious!

Can a friendship lose its meaning? Yes. We can become disconnected. Sadly, I have friends whom I would not be able to find if I wanted to. We have lost touch. I regret that. And it's true in the spiritual life as well. And so, a friendship with Jesus is a relationship that we are called to invest in, to give time toward. It is a gift, but we access the gift through the simple acts of prayer and scripture. To do these simple acts is to stay connected; "I am the vine, you are the branches," he teaches us.

>> **Reflection:** *Take a few minutes to be in silence. How would you describe what it is to be in relationship with Jesus Christ?*

Communion

The teaching of Jesus continues in the form of a command: "Love one another," Jesus says, "as I have loved you" (John 15:12). He repeats these words in verse 17: "Love one another." Love is absolutely at the heart of the gospel—the life, teaching, death, and resurrection of Jesus. I want us to think about love as *communion*, as the experience of community, as Jesus reaching out to people through people. If God is love, then God's people make God's love visible. Again, in John's Gospel there is always something visible, something tangible, about God's love. "For God so loved the world that he gave his only Son" (John 3:16); Jesus, the Word of God, "became flesh and lived among us" (John 1:14).

Years ago, I remember the evangelist John Stott posing a provocative question, one that is even more relevant in our postmodern culture today: "How can the world believe in an invisible God?" The answer, he suggested, is found in 1 John 4:12:

No one has ever seen God; if we love one another,
God lives in us, and [God's] love is perfected in us.

We experience the love of God through God's people! This love is a gift, but each of us must accept it, and this acceptance involves giving up on the idea that I can live the Christian life on my own, without community, apart from communion with others. A few years ago, Robert D. Putnam wrote about the values of our culture in his work *Bowling Alone: The Collapse and Revival of American Community*. The simple thesis of the book is that more people are bowling than ever before, but fewer people are involved in bowling leagues. We are bowling, but we are bowling alone. Increasingly, everything is all about the individual.[1]

On the way to communion, we overcome the obstacle of individualism. We really do need one another. We cannot do it alone. For many, this is the way to salvation, and this was true in my own life. I was impressed, drawn into, overtaken by a small community of Christians who included me and accepted me: a Sunday school class of four people, including the teacher; then a work team that helped to build a storefront church in Brooklyn; a Bible-study group on a college campus; and the quiet witness of people in my own family. My way into the Christian faith came through other Christians. I experienced the *communion* with other people, and then I made the *connection* with God!

>> **Reflection:** *Why might a person be tempted to pursue the spiritual life alone, as an individual?*

>> **Response:** *Try to think of a person who would benefit from an experience of community that is now a blessing to you. How might you extend an invitation?*

The communion with one another happens most often in smaller groups—for example, Sunday school classes; women's circles; Bible studies; clergy covenant groups; and lay participation in Walk to Emmaus reunion groups. I cannot overemphasize the importance of being in a small group. We need a connection with God, but we also need a communion with one another, and the scripture teaches us that we cannot have one without the other. John Wesley shared some insight:

> I shall endeavor to show, that Christianity is
>   essentially a social religion;
> and that to turn it into a solitary religion, is indeed
>   to destroy it.[2]

We are connected. And the life that flows from the vine into the branches is a life of love. We are grafted into each other, into the tree of life, to use another image from scripture; into the body of Christ, to use yet another. I cannot be a Christian without you, and you cannot be a Christian without me. For some reason, God designed it all in just this way. And so, a part of our conversion is into the communion, the body, the believers, the household of God.

>> **Reflection:** *Try to recall two or three deeply meaningful experiences of Christian community you have shared. Why was the experience so significant? How were trust, risk, accountability, and forgiveness present?*

Catherine of Siena was a fourteenth-century Italian spiritual guide who wrote a series of dialogues or visions. In one of them, she reflected on the body of Christ, poured out for her, and on the responsibility we have in receiving that gift. In her vision, God hires workers to labor in the vineyard of the church—we think of Matthew 20 here—each worker has a vineyard—a soul, in which some things are pruned and uprooted, and other things are nurtured. The vines within each person are all engrafted into the One Vine. But then Catherine says,

> Every one is joined to your neighbors' vineyards without any dividing lines. They are so joined together, in fact, that you cannot do good or evil for yourself without doing the same for your neighbors.[3]

The core conviction is our need for a friendship with Jesus. "I am the vine, you are the branches," he teaches his disciples.

We draw our strength, our life, from him: "Apart from me," he says, "you can do nothing." Then the command and invitation that we should "love one another." To state the point negatively, we cannot love Jesus, whom we have never seen, if we do not love our brother or sister, whom we *have* seen. Said positively, we experience the love of God through God's people. Christianity is always incarnational—it takes on human flesh.

>> **For Further Reading and Reflection:** *Find a copy of* The Message *and read Eugene Peterson's translation of the first chapter of John's Gospel. What does it mean that the "word has taken on human flesh and moved into the neighborhood"?*

Calling

Now we conclude with a necessary implication. We are *connected* with God, and we are in *communion* with one another for a larger purpose: a *calling* in the world. "You did not choose me," Jesus says, "but I chose you. And I appointed you to go and bear fruit" (John 15:16).

What does it mean to bear fruit? We can go back to those who heard this teaching for the first time, the disciples of Jesus. They would have heard these words and placed them in their Mediterranean context. The fruit of the vine produces figs, grapes, olives. These finally become food, oils, wine. But vineyards are primarily for the purpose of making wine. I am not an authority on wine. I have close friends who are winemakers, who have reminded me of the old question and answer, "How do you make a little money in the wine business? You start with a *lot* of money!"

It is not accidental that the scriptures are filled with the imagery of vineyards and wine, with the cycles of planting and nurturing and harvesting, with celebrations where wine is freely poured and enjoyed. When those who listened to Jesus heard his references to vineyards and wine, they would have immediately made the connections: the labor, the cultivation, the pruning, the growth, the fruit, the abundance, the feast. In a vineyard, one experiences life in all of its fullness.

And so, Jesus makes the claim, of himself, that he is the vine. "I came that they may have life, and have it abundantly," he had announced to the disciples (John 10:10). To abide in Jesus is to remain connected to him. When we lose that connection, when the branch is severed from the vine, there is no life, no growth, no fruit. "I want you to abide in me," he is saying. "I want you to remain connected to me." Why does he say this?

The reasons go deeper than a personal relationship with Jesus. We remain connected to the vine because that is the way we bear fruit. And here, the inward spiritual grace becomes an outward and visible sign. The natural consequence of a healthy root taking in nutrients is that it produces something wonderful. It bears fruit.

Jesus had been with the disciples for some time—he spent a significant amount of time with just a few people, hidden mostly from the crowds, investing all of this time in twelve people. He was teaching them about friendship with God. He was instructing them in prayer. He was opening the scriptures to them. There were good days and bad days. Do you ever experience life or ministry in this way? Sometimes they got it, and sometimes they did not. Jesus also sensed that there were unhealthy dynamics going on among them. There were struggles over who would sit in the places of power, over whose voice would be heard most clearly—struggles, by the way, that continue to be with the church. And so, he gave them a command and an invitation: "Love one another."

But the call to discipleship in the way of Jesus imagines yet a more expansive outcome. It was always about more than an individual's spiritual life, or a group of people and their love for one another. Jesus wanted the disciples to bear fruit. He wanted their lives to make a difference. How do we measure that? How do we know if we are bearing fruit, if we are making a difference?

I love the insight of Oswald Chambers:

> Our spiritual life cannot be measured by success as the world measures it, but only by what God pours through us.[4]

"*What God pours through us*" . . . I like that. When I hear Jesus say, "I appointed you to go and bear fruit," a word occurs to me: *accountability*. What is important is that we allow the grace of

God to flow through us into the lives of others. I love the words of "The Great Thanksgiving" in the service of Holy Communion:

> Pour out your Holy Spirit on us gathered here,
>   and on these gifts of bread and wine.
> Make them be for us the body and blood of Christ,
> that we may be for the world the body of Christ,
>   redeemed by his blood. (UMH, no. 10)

We allow the inward and spiritual grace to become an outward and visible sign. The wine is to be shared, following the example of Jesus, who said at the Passover feast, "'This is my body that is for you. . . . This cup is the new covenant in my blood'" (1 Cor. 11:24-25).

》 Response: *This week, in some tangible way, seek to make a difference in the life of a person who is outside your circle of friends or community of faith. What unselfish act might be a reflection of Jesus Christ in the world?*

Our calling as disciples of Jesus is to bear fruit. To speak confessionally, a friendship with Jesus is very important to me. I am working on my spiritual life; I am not there yet, but I am working on it. I pray and read the scriptures every day. I need this. I hope that when my ministry comes to a conclusion, others will know this—that I was a person who depended on God. I do.

Love is at the core of what it means to be among the followers of Jesus. Love is about relationships; it is about dignity; it is about integrity; sometimes love is about pruning; and it is about forgiveness. It is my love for you, not my ideal of you, but my love for you as you really are.

This is essential, that we love God and that we love one another; in the Wesleyan tradition this is the definition of *holiness*. But there is more. Beyond a connection with Jesus and a communion with one another, there is calling to bear fruit in the world. What would this fruit look like? It would look like people coming to know Jesus Christ as their Lord and Savior. It would look like new disciples, disciples of all ages, disciples from every nation, transforming their neighborhoods and communities and the world, welcoming children, and especially children of color coming into our churches, rebuilding the ruined cities, justice and righteousness flowing like a mighty stream.

>> **Reflection:** *Where do you see the followers of Jesus bearing fruit in the world? What are the outward and visible signs?*

I once heard the great preacher Zan Holmes say that no message or witness should end without some good news and without giving God the credit. The good news is that we are welcome at the feast, to *connect* with Jesus, to be a part of his *communion*, the disciples, and to respond to his *call* to follow him into a world that hungers and thirsts for the abundant life that he shares.

And if any or all of this is happening, let us give God the credit. How do we do this? "My Father is glorified by this," Jesus says, "that you bear much fruit and become my disciples" (John 15:8).

>> **For Further Reading and Reflection:** *Read Isaiah, chapters 5 and 27. How is your life a "vineyard"? What is God's relationship to and purpose for these vineyards? And how do you attend to the fruitfulness and flourishing of these vineyards?*

The Sower, the Seed, and the Soils

————

Mark 4:1-9

So, a confession, at the outset: I was never really good at gardening. I think I grew a bean once, in a milk carton, in the first grade. My friends watched as their seeds blossomed into healthy beans; mine, not so much, although you could tell it was a bean. For most of our life and ministry, my wife, Pam, and I served churches in Western North Carolina, which is really fertile soil. And yet a mentor told us, early on, that a preacher should never have a garden. "If it is a good year," he said, "you will get everyone else's abundance; and if it is a bad year, you would not be able to grow anything anyway!"

We have a story about a sower and seeds and soil. I feel inadequate to bring any practical expertise to you about it. But I do love this parable of Jesus.

Hardness of Heart

So, as Jesus tells the story, some seed fell on the *path*. I try to walk a couple of miles each day. It is a longtime habit, and it helps me in a variety of ways. I was recently out one morning, and I realized that each day I walk the same route, at times on pavement and at other times on a hard dirt surface. I realized that a seed would never penetrate this kind of ground. So, why does the seed fall there?

When the scriptures speak of hard surfaces, the recurring phrase used is "hardness of heart." This could easily describe me. I may think that I don't have anything to learn from you, because you are a layperson or Pentecostal or Catholic or Jewish, whereas I happen to be United Methodist. Have you ever been there, where it's clear someone has not had your life experience or they vote differently from you or you imagine that they differ from you in a significant way?

>> **Reflection:** *How are we tempted to place others in "boxes" based on our stereotypes or assumptions about their appearance?*

This hardness of heart may be the impediment to the formation of community. We become rigid in our assumptions, in our stereotypes, and then we label one another. And, of course, the hard path can represent our relationship to God. Perhaps we refuse to believe that God would "stoop to our weakness," in the language of the hymn "Spirit of God, Descend upon My Heart." We wonder, *What could God possibly be saying to me? Why would God be speaking to me?* Sometimes our hearts and minds are closed, and it is like a seed hitting the surface of the hard ground.

Shallowness of Spirit

Other seed fell on *rocky ground*, where there was not much soil. This is the danger of a shallow spirituality. This speaks of the shelf life of an enthusiasm that is not sustainable. We go from book to book, fad to fad, expert to expert, self-help project to self-help project. We sometimes speak of thin and thick cultures. Thin cultures are more superficial—there are fewer shared values. A shallow spirituality is also somewhat analogous to what Kenda Creasy Dean, citing the work of the National Study of Youth and Religion, refers to as the inadequacy of the guiding beliefs of "Moralistic Therapeutic Deism":

1. A god exists who created and orders the world and watches over life on earth.
2. God wants people to be good, nice, and fair to each other, as taught in the Bible and by most world religions.
3. The central goal of life is to be happy and to feel good about oneself.
4. God is not involved in my life except when I need God to resolve a problem.
5. Good people go to heaven when they die.[1]

What do you make of this list of guiding beliefs? Do you sense a shallowness or superficiality within and outside our churches?

>> **Reflection:** *Where is God calling you to go deeper in spiritual formation? in community engagement? in study of scripture?*

A Cluttered Life

Other seed fell among soil and was *choked by the thorns.* This is the danger of competing claims for our hearts, minds, and lives. We want to make a place for God in our lives; we make new year's resolutions, but anxieties and fears and desires and ambitions seep in, and they suck up all of the nutrients, namely our time, our talents, or our treasure. And there is little space available for the life of the spirit.

In many of our experiences of church, the elements that choke the life of the spirit are a pervasive "hermeneutic of suspicion."[2] In a church culture, a hermeneutic of suspicion began with a default critique of what was perceived to be a mainline church aligned with the powers of the world. That was Christendom, and the assumptions of many of our seminary professors and much of the media presume this as our context.

The problem that emerges with a hermeneutic of suspicion is that we no longer live in a church culture. Ours is a post-Christian culture. This is the insight that is giving birth to new forms of church and is increasingly a more realistic way of seeing our own context. So how do we move from a hermeneutic of suspicion to a "hermeneutic of generativity"?[3] How can we transition from diagnosing scripture to allowing scripture to lead us into both self-examination and gratitude?

There is surely, in these first three kinds of soils, failure and success, perseverance and experimentation. And most of us, if we are honest, are a mixture of soils, hardened and shallow and filled with a variety of thorns. We have all experienced *hardness of heart*, and a *shallow spirituality*, and a *cluttered life*. And yet, there is another outcome.

Good Soil

The seed is planted in good soil, and it brings forth an abundance beyond our dreams or imagination! This is the blessing of fruitfulness. But let us quickly acknowledge that this is not our work, nothing we boast about. The soil is simply the composition of everything that has flowed into our lives: advantages and opportunities and privileges, blessings and provisions and grace. Our pride is the sin of taking credit for something that God has actually done for us. As the apostle Paul wrote in 1 Corinthians 3:6, "I planted, Apollos watered, but God gave the growth."

To be the good soil is not our achievement. It is more about being receptive to the gospel. The good soil is creating the conditions that make us more holy and more mature. To be holy in the Wesleyan tradition is to love God and our neighbor. And holiness and maturity are generative. Aside from anything else in life, this is the calling of an adult, a leader, a Christian: to be generative. This is mentoring; this is discipleship.

>> **Reflection:** *Try to think of a mentor who has guided you in your walk with God. How has God used you as a mentor in the life of someone else?*

Discipleship is the good soil; it is Bible study and prayer and being in a small group and doing justice and loving mercy and walking humbly with God. Discipleship includes what we do on Sunday—indeed it is essential. But it is also what we do on the other six days—indeed what we do with our entire lives. And discipleship is a process that is lifelong.

Four Seasons

I was a pastor in the local church for twenty-eight years, and I loved that life. I often look back and give thanks for particular people who were my teachers in those churches. One experience is relevant here. I had been in Haiti on a short-term mission. I returned, came down with an illness related to an infectious disease, and I was hospitalized. I received excellent medical care, and soon I was better. I did, however, miss a Sunday at church, so the congregation knew this and prayed for me.

Later in the winter, I was visiting a friend in the hospital. He was a member of the church. His name was John, and he was a physician. And when I went into his room, he greeted me with the words, "So, you picked up something in Haiti!" His son, sitting in the corner of the room, became interested. We talked, and it turned out John's son worked as a scientist with the Centers for Disease Control.

Well, I came to know John and, over time, his other two sons as well. I learned that John, the father, was a very wise man who had three accomplished sons—one a scientist in Atlanta, another a law professor in Virginia, and the third an architect in Nashville. In his last years, John created a fund and brought his sons to see him on the same weekend, about three times each year, to spend time together. He was teaching them to work with one another and to be a family again after he had passed.

Well, time passed, and John died the next fall. We planned his funeral, and in that church, we had a tradition that we called a "family witness." The son who was a law professor gave the family witness, although I think he and his brothers collaborated. And that witness was so well crafted, that I remember it as if I had heard it this week. He said a person has four seasons in this life.

- There is *a time to learn*, and so he talked about John's years of study to become a physician.

- There is *a time to do*, and here he reflected on John's practice of medicine and the way he had blessed his patients and coworkers.
- There is *a time to teach others*. John had been a guide to other physicians, and indeed he had mentored his sons. His son talked about his father's faith.
- And there is *a time to be*. John had reached the place where he took pleasure simply in being in the presence of people he loved.

>> **Reflection:** *What would you consider to be the present "season" in your own life? What sort of progression of service and influence do you see in the lives of others?*

The Seasons of Our Lives

A sower went forth to plant a seed. In life, there are cycles of planting and growing and harvesting. And, of course, the imaginative power of these parables of Jesus is that they speak to us in different seasons of our lives and in different ways. Surely, we have been the hard ground that God's love could not penetrate. We have been enthusiastic about something, but we soon lost passion and energy. Or we found a focus, and then the worries and concerns of the world distracted us. We have all been there.

And then, at times, and all by God's grace, we have been the good soil. God blessed us; God blessed others through us. It is prideful to take any credit for that. "I planted, Apollos watered, but God gave the growth" (1 Corinthians 3:6). The apostle Paul was right: I have been the beneficiary, over and over again, of the abundances of others.

There are seasons of our lives, to learn, to do, to teach others, to be. John had lived through those seasons, and he had lived long enough to see the fruit of his labors. He struck me as a wise man, one who listened to his life and who, in the words of Jesus, had "ears to hear" (Matt. 11:15, NKJV). That is wisdom. In the parables, Jesus is a wisdom teacher. And wisdom is learning, we hope, from the mistakes we have made, from the harm we have done to others, and from the harm that has been done to us. Wisdom is seeking to be the good soil that bears fruit.

Generative Soil

So, why do you think Jesus taught this parable? Yes, northern Galilee is a richly agricultural area, and I have been blessed to travel in that region. But it went beyond that: The sower, the seed, and the soils pointed to something greater. Jesus actually explains the meaning of it in private, later in Mark 4.

It is counterintuitive, because we often think that spiritual growth depends on having the right teacher or the charismatic preacher or the extraordinary leader or just the right book. (And thank God for any of these gifts when they come along.) But Jesus is counterintuitive in that he shifts the responsibility to us.

The seed is the Word of God; that never changes, but it matters where it is planted. In the parable, it is all about the quality of the soil and, finally, our receptivity to the gospel.

So, can we make the transition from hardness of heart and shallowness of spirit and a cluttered life to the rhythm of learning, doing, teaching others, and being? Can we be generative, growing Christians who multiply our blessings in the lives of others, who disciple the next generations? Can we, together, be a church of the good soil?

I invite you into the words of this prayer, which calls us to a greater receptivity to the gifts of God in the complicated and challenging places where we live:

> What we cannot fix, you salvage.
> What we cannot endure, you absorb.
> What we cannot overcome, you bridge.
> What we cannot cure, you heal.
> What we cannot imagine, you envision.
> What we cannot confront, you convict.
> What we cannot forgive, you restore.
> What we cannot produce, you create.
> What we cannot withhold, you accept.
> What we cannot love, you embrace.
> What we cannot speak, you hear.
> What we cannot complete, you perfect.[4]

Amen.

>> **For Further Reading and Reflection:** *See the classic work on adult development* The Seasons of a Man's Life *by Daniel J. Levinson and Carol Gilligan's research from* In a Different Voice, *which maps the unique experiences of women. To learn more about Christian maturity among youth and adults, see Kenda Creasy Dean's* Almost Christian.

The Feeding of the Multitudes

———

Luke 9:10-17

At the heart of the biblical story is a meal. Israel tells its story at the Passover meal, one of deliverance from slavery and entrance into the Promised Land (see Exodus 12). Jesus shares this Passover meal with his own disciples (see John 13) and commands them to eat this meal in remembrance of him (see Matthew 26). Jesus feeds the multitudes (see John 6), eats with sinners (see Luke 15), and shares a mysterious meal with two of the disciples on the way to Emmaus (see Luke 24). The first Christians break bread together with glad and generous hearts (see Acts 2). Later, there are abuses in the practice of the Lord's Supper (see 1 Corinthians 11). One of the most misunderstood concepts in Christian faith and practice, the reference to eating the Lord's Supper in an unworthy manner, referred to the experiences of gluttony and poverty at the common meal. The

Christian hope was also shaped by the expectation of a Messiah who would preside over a great banquet (see Luke 14).

>> **For Further Reading and Reflection:** *Look up at least two of the above passages—John 6 and 1 Corinthians 11, for example. How are these contexts different? Why do the different contexts matter?*

At the heart of the biblical story is a meal. Yet many Christians misunderstand what is happening here, or they avoid Communion, or they see it as an optional experience for a follower of Jesus. Think of this study as an explanation of the holy meal (Communion, the Eucharist, the Lord's Supper), what we receive in this meal, what's on the menu, and why.

It helps to connect this meal to our common experiences. Family meals can take on different connotations; sometimes there is a special occasion, sometimes a sense of urgency; and at other times, the meal is a common experience of nourishment and sustenance. Think about the truly significant meals across the span of your life. A few come to mind for me. As a teenager, I ate many meals at my grandmother's home. She was an amazing cook, and I was a voracious eater! When my wife and I were dating, we had one of those coupon books—we were students with almost no money, and so we would eat wherever we could find a "buy one, get one free" meal. There were some terrible meals along the way, but it didn't really matter—we were together. I think of our wedding rehearsal dinner: The venue we had selected burned to the ground ten days before our wedding! Once we got over the shock, we finally had the meal in my wife's parents' home.

I think of other meals that, in hindsight, were also unique. Our older daughter's best friend in high school and college is of the Muslim faith. We had dinner, our family and her family, at a Chinese restaurant in Chapel Hill, North Carolina, and at a Thai restaurant in Charlotte. A year later, her father, who was my age, died unexpectedly. I think of a meal in Jerusalem with a conservative Jewish family on the sabbath and another with a community of Palestinian Christians in Bethlehem, just a few miles in geographical distance but a universe away. I think of the meal we had for our younger daughter at a club that overlooked the skyline of the city on the day she graduated from high school.

>> **Reflection:** *Try to recall two or three significant meals from your own experience. In your remembrance, what do you see, hear, and smell? What are the sights, sounds, and aromas?*

Meals are the occasions for many of life's richest experiences. This is true for the Christian and the practice of faith. "Do this," Jesus said, "in remembrance of me." And so, we eat this meal together. But what is really happening?

I was a local church pastor for almost thirty years. At the conclusion of worship services, I would often say, "Communion draws us closer to God and closer to one another." Communion has a vertical dimension and a horizontal dimension. The vertical dimension has to do with grace. Holy Communion is a sacrament for us, an outward and visible sign of an inward and spiritual grace. What is *grace*? Something we did not earn, something we do not deserve, something we can never repay. And so, those who take Communion are not the deserving, those who have it all together. Those who take Communion are hungry and thirsty for love, for grace, for God. That is the lesson from the prophet Isaiah. "You're invited, come, sit down at the table, it has been set for you," and then, "Put that money away!" It is as if God is saying, "Your money's no good here, you could not afford this meal, and besides, I have made you a part of the family."

That's *grace*, the vertical dimension of Communion: something we did not earn, something we do not deserve, something we can never repay. So, it is a meal, but it is a meal that we eat *together*. It is spiritual, but it is also social; it is vertical, but it is also horizontal. And so, we come together, we kneel together, we confess together, we receive together.

At the conclusion of worship, I would often ask the congregation to join hands; Communion draws us closer to one another. There is a wonderful image of a wheel—as the spokes come nearer to the center, they are in closer relationship to one another. And this too is the grace of God, for we need human community. Someone commented to me, in the midst of the heightened national media focus on an infectious disease, that some churches were bypassing the joining of hands in worship, the passing of the peace, and even Communion itself. In that same week, a member of our church told me that since her husband had passed away a few years ago, she often goes days without touching another human being, and to grasp the hand of a friend beside her in worship is not something that she takes for granted. It is a blessing.

>> **Response:** *How often do you eat meals alone? How often do you share meals with others? How might you invite a new person in your workplace or community to share a meal with you this week? What are the obstacles to such an invitation, and what might be a benefit?*

An additional word about the horizontal / social dimensions of the meal: It was very clear in the Gospels that Jesus ate with sinners. He was criticized for this very reason at the beginning of Luke 15, and this occasioned three parables—the parable of the lost sheep, the parable of the lost coin, and the parable of the lost (or prodigal) son. The Wesleyan tradition grasps this in the hymn of Charles Wesley,

> Come, sinners, to the gospel feast,
> let every soul be Jesus' guest.

And so, Methodist Christians practice open Communion: If you feel led to receive the grace of God (that's the vertical part), and if you will seek to live in peace with your neighbor (that's the horizontal part), you are welcome, just as you are.

Communion is a meal. It is God's providence, sustenance, and grace; it is a meal that we share together; and it has a larger purpose. Throughout my life, I have often heard a common prayer, one spoken in the contexts of fellowship dinners, and usually by members of the church who are generally less wordy than preacher types! The prayer might go something like this: "Bless this food for our use and us in Thy service." I have heard some variation of this prayer all my life. Sometimes an additional phrase is added: "Bless this food for our use and us in Thy service, *and make us mindful of the needs of others.*" So, what is the larger purpose? The meal is not only for us, the meal has been prepared for all. Again, the Communion hymn of Charles Wesley:

> Come, sinners, to the gospel feast,
> let every soul be Jesus' guest.
> Ye need not one be left behind,
> for God hath bid all humankind. (UMH, no. 616)

Or we can go back farther in the tradition, to a story about a hungry crowd, the disciples who wanted to send them away, Jesus' comment, "You give them something to eat," and the appeal to a little boy, "What do you have in your basket?"

Five loaves, two fish . . . this turns out to be sufficient for the multitudes, and the lesson is clear: God's grace is available to all and sufficient for all. And this is our mission: to connect the love and grace that we find here with the world. In the Great Thanksgiving, we say, about the elements of Holy Communion:

Make them be for us the body and blood of Christ,
that we may be for the world the body of Christ,
redeemed by his blood. (UMH, no. 10)

The gospel describes the human reality that the guest list is enormous, but not all accept the invitation. We live in a culture that views worship in general, and Holy Communion in particular, as an option. And so a scriptural imagination develops a friendly argument with a culture—and it is present inside the church—that has marginalized the experience of Communion for a variety of reasons: We do not feel spiritual or we know that we are imperfect or we simply do not have the time. It is true that many of us are overwhelmed, and yet we are also undernourished.

>> **Reflection:** *Spend time in silence. How are you overwhelmed? And how are you also undernourished? How can accountability and vulnerability help in finding a new and more sustainable way of living?*

In a culture that hungers for the Spirit, we have not maintained the centrality of the Table as the source of life-giving food for the soul. We have allowed our spiritual lives to become isolated from the body of Christ that sustains it, and we have become anemic in our response to the great challenges of the world. The Table is a reminder of our human need for communion with God and with one another, so that we might engage with the world that also needs this grace.

It is a busy week, and I do not have an appointment for lunch. So, I gather some work and drive a couple of minutes to a nearby restaurant. I know the staff and they know me, and I order my usual: unsweetened tea with lemon, a Reuben sandwich, and a cup of the soup of the day. They take the order, bring the tea. I get involved in my work, the Sunday sermon, the calendar, the to-do list. I get more involved in it. The time is passing, but it is fine, it is quiet, and they refill my tea. I am thinking about a meeting that is in the not-too distant future, but I am also thinking, *I have really been here a long time!*

Then I look up from my notebook and realize that there is a bill for the lunch. There is one problem: The meal never came! So, I walk over and get someone's attention: "I'm not sure what happened . . . my food never came." They are extremely embarrassed and profusely apologetic. "It's really not a huge problem," I say. They are trying to figure out what has happened, and I am saying, "I would still like to eat lunch while I am here!"

The waiter brings the soup and quickly the Reuben, and he will not let me pay. Then the manager comes by and gives me a card for two dinners there in the evening. I tell them it's not necessary, I go there often, it's not a big deal. Being the cheap person that I am, I am also thinking, *This is turning out pretty good!* I did leave a much more substantial tip than usual, and my wife and I enjoyed dinner there one evening the next week.

I share this to confess that what we do together in corporate worship is important, to be prepared for guests, to be prepared with music, to be prepared in prayer and with the words that are spoken. In our culture, people are hungry and thirsty for something, and they do not always find it in the church. The vertical dimension: That is between the individual and God, and so we ask, in prayer, for the outpouring of the Spirit on us and on the gifts of bread and wine that are placed on the table.

But the horizontal dimension—that is within our power. And this makes all the difference when we welcome—or, better yet, when we invite—someone we know to share a meal with us or to share the meal that is Holy Communion with us. When we do this, we are creating a space where our greatest gift and our most compelling need come together.

We have been invited, all of us, to a great feast. When we commune, we are in a relationship with God, through Jesus Christ. That's grace. When we commune, we are not alone; we come with others, other sinners. That's community. And if we have met God in this meal, if we have met one another in this meal, we then go out into the world as different people, more aware of the faithfulness of God, more connected and less isolated, and, yes, more mindful of the needs of others.

Earlier in this chapter I mentioned a common prayer that I had heard in fellowship meals, drawn from a life of experiences in local churches. From young adulthood I began to serve with mission teams, many of them in Latin American contexts. And around meals with these brothers and sisters, I began to hear yet another simple and profoundly moving prayer:

> To those who hunger, give bread;
> to those who have bread, give a hunger for justice.

A life in communion with God is one that is also lived in communion with one another. And as John wrote in one of his letters, we cannot love God, whom we have never seen, if we do not love our brother or sister whom we have seen. We hunger for bread and the bread of life. We grow in the desire for spirituality and justice. A scriptural imagination helps us to see that bread is always more than bread, that communion is life with God and with one another. The One who feeds the multitudes feeds us also and calls us to feed others.

>> **For Further Reading and Reflection:** *Do some research on the indicators of hunger in your community. Read Exodus 16, John 6, and Luke 24. Learn more about the model of "dinner church," which is a new movement centered on gathering for a meal as a form of worship. If you often eat alone, plan to share a meal this week with a friend or coworker.*

The Parable of the Talents

Matthew 25:14-30, CEB

We refer to the story that Jesus tells in Matthew 25 as the parable of the talents. *Talent* is an unfortunately misleading word. We think of talent as a skill, an ability. When we think of talent, we think of athletes like Stephen Curry or Serena Williams; or poets like Mary Oliver and Billy Collins; or musicians such as Alison Krauss or Bono or Ray Charles or Yo-Yo Ma. Or maybe we think of people closer by: "She does this well"; "He is good at this."

In the ancient world, those listening to Jesus would have known that a *talent* was the approximate value of fifteen years of wages, a substantial sum of money. In the story, a man is leaving on a journey, and he gives each of his servants a gift. One servant receives five talents, one receives two talents, and the last servant receives one talent.

Each is entrusted with something that is significant, and each receives a different sum. The distribution is neither even nor fair. As with other stories Jesus told—the workers in the vineyard, for one, where everyone is paid the same but for differing amounts of work—this is not about fairness. It is in reference to a gift that we do not deserve or earn.

>> **Reflection:** *In your own life, workplace, or community, where do you observe the realities of unfairness? Describe two or three examples.*

The gospel, someone has said, is not good advice; it is, literally, good news, and so we begin with grace, not law; with gift, not obligation. We begin with an appreciative inquiry into our assets, strengths, and talents. Or to frame it theologically, we reflect on the prevenient grace of God, gifts that go before our responses.

In the parable, the resources belong to the master, who goes away, and the servants are left to work out for themselves what they will do with these gifts. A church that I served for many years (Providence United Methodist in Charlotte, North Carolina) has had the blessing of being in Haiti for more than forty years in a partnership and friendship. There is a medical clinic; Jesus was a healer. There is a school; Jesus was a teacher. There is an emerging microcredit partnership, and Jesus is in that as well.

For two years, a young man from Haiti named Jacques lived with us. He is now a medical student. We often talked about Haitian proverbs. One that I came across went this way: "God gives but does not share." "Jaqcues," I asked, "what do you think this means?" He chose his words carefully, as he always did. Then he spoke: "God gives us everything, but we have to work out how to distribute it for everyone. God gives, but it is up to us to share."

On a hillside in the Galilee, a boy had a basket with five loaves of bread and two fish. These were the gifts of God amidst a hungry gathering of seekers. "Send them away," the disciples advised Jesus. "You give them something to eat," he responded. God gives but does not share; that part is up to us. When Christians gather to celebrate the Eucharist, the Great Thanksgiving, with the bread and wine placed on the table, we say these words:

> Make them be for us the body and blood of Christ,
> that we may be for the world the body of Christ,
>   redeemed by his blood. (UMH, no. 10)

It helps to remember that the gospel transforms the world; indeed, that the gospel, in the language of the Magnificat (see Luke 1), has already transformed the world. This is the gift. The wisdom in that beautiful proverb Haitians say to one another is that everything is a gift from God, and yet God leaves the details of distribution up to us. God gives but does not share.

The gifts belong to the Master, and these are God's to give. I do know this: From the perspective of the world, this planet that we share with more than seven billion other people, most of us have received a very generous harvest of talents. The investor and philanthropist Warren Buffett is said to have commented once to someone who had made a fortune, "You're not a genius, you were just born at the right time and in the right place!" Malcolm Gladwell, in his book *Outliers*, notes that most of those who are successful are "grounded in a web of advantages and inheritances, some deserved, some not, some earned, some just plain lucky—but all critical to making [us] who [we] are."[1]

>> **Reflection:** *What does the word* privilege *mean to you? to society? How do followers of Jesus see their privileges in unique ways?*

And so, the master in the parable gives. Why does one servant receive five, and one two, and one *one*? The master gives to each "according to [her] ability" (Matt. 25:15). Sometimes we are ready to receive a gift, and sometimes we are not. Jesus told other stories about this as well. Some people were invited to a party, but they declined. "We are too busy," they said, "please ask us again." Others were invited, and these replied, "Please keep us on the guest list, but for now, we cannot accept." Please ask us again." The Master gives according to the receptivity and ability of the recipient. As Augustine said,

"God is always trying to give good things to us,
   but our hands are too full to receive them."

The story of the parable moves on, and we shift our focus from the master, who has now left the scene, to the servants. We move from gift to response, from blessing to responsibility. In the same way that the talents are not distributed uniformly, the servants' responses are not all alike. The one who is given five doubles her share. The one who is given two doubles the portion as well. The third servant, the one who receives one talent, buries his in the ground. At some point, a great time later, the master returns to settle accounts. There will be a judgment, an accounting that we will give to the One who is giver of all things. Call it an audit. Why? Because the talents originally came from the master, who wants to know how it has gone.

To the one whose five talents became ten, the master says, "Well done." To the one whose two talents have become four, the master says, "Well done." To both of these servants, the master says, "You have been faithful over a little, I will set you over much; enter into the joy of your master."

"You have been faithful over *a little*." It is interesting, in that five talents—seventy-five years' wages; and two talents—thirty years' wages—was not really "a little." It is also significant that two of the servants respond to the receipt of their gifts with creativity and faithfulness. In the way the story gets told, we do dwell on the third servant, but the first two multiply their gifts. "Well done," the master says.

Now, the third servant: He comes before the master, and he offers a justification for his behavior, the reason why he has buried his talent in the ground: "I knew you were a harsh master, and I was afraid." What we think about the Master, what we think about God, shapes what we will do with our gifts. And what we think about God shapes what we believe about human nature.

Here is the crucial question: Do you think people are basically selfish and stingy or generous and gracious? I first heard this question posed by one of my mentors, Kennon Callahan. If you think we are basically selfish and stingy, then giving is a great challenge; it is unnatural; it is manipulating us to do something that is against our nature. But we as Christians believe that we have been created in the image of God, which leads to another question: What is God like?

"I knew you were a harsh master," the servant blurts out, "and I was afraid." The servant's response is rooted in fear, grounded in a flawed understanding of God (who is Love and whose love casts out fear) and an equally flawed vision of neighbor. One of Jesus' most memorable stories was a parable inspired by a simple question: "Who is my neighbor?" (see Luke 10:25-37).

I mentioned Jaqcues, a native of Haiti, who was a reminder to me that the Haitian people are our neighbors. Jeffrey Sachs, an economist at Columbia University, reflected years after the 2010 earthquake that caused such great devastation there about the general question of how Haiti is doing and what needs to happen next, and he focused more specifically on the question of development in the nation of Haiti. He noted that Haiti had been plagued by a development policy that had not matched the aspirations of the people, and for this reason, it had failed. Factories were built in one major city, Port-au-Prince, and when the capital markets shifted, the resources had dried up, the jobs had disappeared, and the people had become destitute.

Sachs noted that Haiti is in need of a development policy that matches the aspirations of her people. What are those aspirations? Education. Food. Health. And I would also add the gospel.

In prior centuries, when missionaries went into the countries of the world, they were often allowed in because of these skills. A medical doctor or a nurse. A teacher. An agricultural specialist. On a mission field, these resources often make the difference between life and death.

Those of us who live in North America in the twenty-first century have been planted in a mission field. Many do not have access to a basic education, really. Or to food on the weekends, if they are poor students. Or, increasingly, to health care. And many find themselves spiritually hungry. In the face of expansive human needs, our response can often echo the disciples of Jesus' day; we are tempted to say also to the Lord, "You give them something to eat!"

As we enter into the parable of Jesus, we reflect on our own gifts, talents, and abilities, and we are more aware that we are grounded in a web of advantages and inheritances.

The preacher Tony Campolo noted a sociological study in which fifty people over the age of ninety-five were asked a question: "If you could live your life over again, what you would do differently?" There were three primary responses:

- "I would reflect more."
- "I would risk more."
- "I would do more things that would live on after I am dead."[2]

"What would you do differently?" That is almost the question the master asks the three servants when he returns.

To share our gifts is to take a risk. As Christians, we know that our sharing is grounded in relation to One who has shared deeply and profoundly with us, in sending the incarnate Jesus to be our Savior. That is the risk of the incarnation. The aspirations that our Creator has for us, in the word made flesh, have become operational.

At a basic level, our identification with this God implies that we take the name *Christian* in baptism, which says less about our own merit or goodness and more about our awareness that all that we are and have and aspire to be is a gift; it is grace.

And our identification with this God implies a risk that we take for the sake of others. We open our baskets and share the bread and the fish; we open our homes and welcome the stranger; we open our table to welcome all who hunger and thirst for justice and righteousness. As followers of Jesus, we take our web of advantages and inheritances and extend them, as the great theologian, educator, and civil rights leader Howard Thurman would insist, to the "disinherited."

The parable of the talents does end on something of a downer, in "the outer darkness" with "weeping and gnashing of teeth" (v. 30). It would be possible to gloss over that, to ignore it—such a stark ending—and yet it may be the storyteller's way of getting our attention, keeping us awake. There is much at stake; it is a question of life and death—our gifts, our talents, our financial resources, our abilities have the power to bless or curse. They can be instruments of light or darkness.

God gives—this is the good news. But God does not share. God leaves that up to us, to you and me.

Let us respond, let us give, and let us enter into the joy of our Master.

>> **For Further Reading and Reflection:** *Learn more about community-based asset mapping. Read* Christian Social Innovation: Renewing Wesleyan Witness, *by L. Gregory Jones. If you are Anglo, seek to learn more about white privilege.*

Next Steps

In developing this resource, I envisioned a number of settings where women and men might gather to pray; study; form community; and see themselves, the scriptures, and their communities in new ways. These are a few of those contexts:

- Fresh Expressions of Church
- Cohorts of Young Adults in Communities (such as *Generation Transformation, Young Adult Mission Movement*)
- Campus Ministry Small Groups
- Missional Wisdom House Churches
- Leadership Academies for New Church Planters
- Nehemiah (Legacy) Churches
- Houses of Studies in Theological Schools
- Covenant Groups
- Lay Seminary Participants
- Short-Term Mission Teams
- Design Thinking Experiences and Cohorts

I would recommend the following as resources that might help you to grow as a disciple:

- Catherine of Siena, *The Dialogue*
- Dietrich Bonhoeffer, *Life Together*
- *The Imitation of Christ: Selections Annotated and Explained*, Thomas à Kempis, annotation by Paul Wesley Chilcote
- Howard Thurman, *Jesus and the Disinherited*
- Henri J. M. Nouwen, *In the Name of Jesus: Reflections on Christian Leadership*
- Evelyn Underhill, *Practical Mysticism: A Little Book for Normal People*
- Laceye and Gaston Warner, *From Relief to Empowerment: How Your Church Can Cultivate Sustainable Mission*

For resources that point to new (but at times also ancient) ways of forming communities of disciples, I commend the following, and especially for those called into leadership:

- Graham Cray, *Mission-Shaped Church: Church Planting and Fresh Expressions of Church in a Changing Context*
- Kenda Creasy Dean, *Almost Christian: What the Faith of Our Teenagers Is Telling the American Church*
- Elaine A. Heath and Scott T. Kisker, *Longing for Spring: A New Vision for Wesleyan Community*
- Michael Frost and Allen Hirsch, *The Shaping of Things to Come: Innovation and Mission for the 21st-Century Church*

- Kenneth H. Carter Jr. and Audrey Warren, *Fresh Expressions: A New Kind of Methodist Church for People Not in Church*

And if you want to go deeper into the Gospels, I offer an admittedly subjective short list of commentaries for those called to the ministry of teaching with a motivation toward more serious study:

- Mortimer Arias, *Announcing the Reign of God: Evangelization and the Subversive Memory of Jesus*
- Stanley Hauerwas, *Matthew* (Brazos Theological Commentary on the Bible)
- C. Clifton Black, *Mark* (Abingdon New Testament Commentaries)
- Luke Timothy Johnson, *The Gospel of Luke* (Sacra Pagina Series)
- Amy-Jill Levine, *Short Stories by Jesus: The Enigmatic Parables of a Controversial Rabbi*
- Lesslie Newbigin, *The Light Has Come: An Exposition of the Fourth Gospel*
- Raymond Brown, *The Gospel According to John* (Anchor Bible Series), two volumes
- Marianne Meye Thompson, *John: A Commentary (The New Testament Library)*

Acknowledgments

———

I am grateful to Tim Moore and Doug Ruffle, who were con-versation partners with me at an earlier stage and helped me to see the potential for this book. This resource, although brief, is an expression of a lifetime of teaching and preaching these texts in particular contexts. Each of the contexts reminds me of friends, mentors, and congregations along the way. My attention to John 15 began as the founding pastor of St. Timothy's United Methodist Church in Greensboro, North Carolina. I was blessed by lively conversations there with Professor Barnes Tatum, a charter member of that church and himself a renowned scholar of the New Testament. Later, I would use this as the text in the service of installation as resident bishop of the Florida Annual Conference, in a sermon preached at First United Methodist Church in Lakeland.

The reflection on Mark 4 and generativity arose from par-ticipation in a cohort group led by Craig Robertson of Spiritual Leadership Inc., and then in a sermon preached by Rev. Leslie Griffiths at City Road Methodist Church in London, England, in a Wesley Heritage Pilgrimage of Florida Conference clergy and spouses led by Jorge and Cheryl Acevedo. The connection of these two experiences led me to work on this passage through the winter and spring, and then to offer the sermon at the Florida Annual Conference session that summer. A preacher does not often have the time or occasion to till the same small plot of scripture for months, but I did, and I am grateful. I have long ago asked forgiveness for those who heard these sermons more than once!

The feeding of the five thousand in Luke 9 began as a sermon preached at Providence United Methodist Church in Charlotte, North Carolina. I served that congregation for eight years, and the Eucharist was a central and core activity of our life together, as was sharing meals with members and friends in that church, and as was, in addition, taking part in initiatives to feed the hungry. Those eight years included significant attention to a major indebtedness (for previously constructed buildings), responding to the 2010 earthquake in Haiti (which my wife, Pam, experienced while serving in Port-au-Prince), and living through the economic meltdown of 2008 at the epicenter of a global banking city. We learned again and again the lessons of abundance amidst seeming scarcity and provision when all seemed uncertain. I loved this congregation and the basic gathering around Word and Table.

I preached on the parable of the talents (Matthew 25) in the glorious Marsh Chapel on the campus of Boston University at the gracious invitation of its dean, Bob Hill.

When I first began to immerse myself in the life and literature of the Fresh Expressions movement in England, my friend Martyn Atkins reminded me that the term "mixed economy of church" was being replaced by the more organic "mixed ecology of church." This led me to begin to connect four passages that speak of organic life, growth, and connection. I have benefited greatly from the missiological genius of the Fresh Expressions movement and, in particular, its analysis of our western post-Christian context and what this means for next generations of disciples of Jesus. I am grateful to the Florida Annual Conference team, Dan Jackson, Michael Beck, Heather Evans, and Caitlin White; and to Audrey Warren, who helped to initiate this work in Florida.

Mostly, I am indebted to those who love the scriptures and are open to life-giving conversations about them, wherever these might happen, with friends, neighbors, and strangers. The promise of God through the scriptures remains true: Jesus is the bread who comes down from heaven and gives life to the world (see John 6:33).

Notes

Introduction

1. Fresh Expressions US website, https://freshexpressionsus.org/2016/09/12/fresh-expressions-101-next/.
2. Ellen F. Davis and Richard B. Hays, "Beyond Criticism: Learning to Read the Bible Again," *The Christian Century* (April 20, 2004), 26.
3. "The Formation of Scriptural Imagination and the Renewal of the Church: A Panel Discussion with Richard Hays, Ellen Davis, and Stanley Hauerwas," *Divinity* 12, no. 2 (Spring 2013): 31.
4. C. Kavin Rowe, "The Formation of Scriptural Imagination," *Divinity* 12, no. 2 (Spring 2013): 8–9.
5. C. Kavin Rowe, "The Formation of Scriptural Imagination," 6.

Chapter 1

1. Robert D. Putnam, *Bowling Alone: The Collapse and Revival of American Community* (New York: Simon & Schuster, 2000).
2. John Wesley, Sermon 24, "Upon Our Lord's Sermon on the Mount," Discourse 4.
3. Wendy M. Wright, *The Rising: Living the Mysteries of Lent, Easter, and Pentecost* (Nashville, TN: Upper Room Books, 1994), 152–53; quoting from Catherine of Siena, *The Dialogue*, translation by Suzanne

Noffke (New York: Paulist Press, 1980), 12. As noted in the endnotes of Wright, "Her [Catherine of Siena's] friend and confessor Raymond of Capua is quoted here."
4. Oswald Chambers, "A Life of Pure and Holy Sacrifice," daily reading for September 2 from *My Utmost for His Highest*, Updated Edition in Today's Language (Grand Rapids, MI: Discovery House, 2017).

Chapter 2

1. Kenda Creasy Dean, "Guiding Beliefs of Moralistic Therapeutic Deism," *Almost Christian: What the Faith of Our Teenagers Is Telling the Church* (Oxford, England, UK: Oxford University Press, 2010), 14.
2. The phrase "hermeneutic of suspicion" is associated with the philosopher Jean Paul Gustave Ricoeur and has influenced work in theological and biblical studies.
3. Susannah Ticciati, "Anachronism or Illumination? Genesis 1 and Creation ex nihilo," *Anglican Theological Review* 99, no. 4 (October 2017): 691–712.
4. Copyright © Kenneth H. Carter Jr.

Chapter 4

1. Malcolm Gladwell, *Outliers: The Story of Success* (New York: Little, Brown, and Company, 2008), 285.
2. Tony Campolo, *Who Switched the Price Tags?* (Nashville, TN: Royal Publishers Inc., 1987), 28–29.